INSIDER'S GUIDE FOR RETURNING VETERANS

Michael B. Wood
Missouri State University

Bedford/St. Martin's   Boston ◆ New York

Manufactured in the United States of America

8   7   6   5   4   3
f   e   d   c   b   a

For information, write: Bedford/St. Martin's, 75 Arlington Street, Boston, MA 02116 (617-399-4000)

ISBN 978-1-4576-5384-1

Contents

INSIDER'S GUIDE
FOR RETURNING VETERANS

Welcome back! You've served your country honorably and have decided to either begin your college experience or return to college after a deployment. Your new mission is to earn your degree, and your educational journey will be an exciting one. As a veteran you bring some great skills you can use as you begin college. You bring an ability to focus on the most important task at hand, as well as a strong work ethic. You are probably goal-oriented and are used to working as part of a team to get the job done. These skills and traits will help you throughout your college career.

You should know up front, though, college might be challenging at times. You may feel that you don't really fit in with the other students in your classes. If you're just starting college, you may be a few years older than the other students and may worry that you're already behind. It's important to know that universities and colleges serve many types of students, including nontraditional adult learners like you. A nontraditional student is generally defined as someone twenty-two years old or older or as anyone who didn't take a direct path from high school to college. In fact, nontraditional students are among the fastest-growing student demographic in the nation. So you are definitely not alone. There's also a possibility that if you are working with the Nontraditional/Adult Student Services office, you feel like you don't really belong there either because of your unique life experiences in the military. Don't worry! This is normal for many returning veteran students—in fact, identity issues are one of the most commonly reported challenges by new veteran students.

If you have any feelings of disconnect, there are many things you can do to overcome these feelings. First, it often helps to connect and communicate with faculty and peers on campus. We'll look at ways to do this later in this guide. Second, you'll want to take advantage of the many services available to returning veterans. You may have more responsibilities than a typical student, and possibly some physical or mental health issues that present additional challenges. The good news is since veterans are beginning or returning to college in large numbers, many college campuses either already have (or are developing) specialized student support services for veterans. Taking advantage of these services and resources is important as you begin your path to earning your degree.

As a veteran student, you may need to work extra hard to overcome some of your past life experiences to ensure you will be successful in college, but you can do it! This guide is intended to help you get squared away and on the right track to college success.

Transitioning Into College

Part of transitioning successfully into college is realizing that you are not alone. Below is a list of common challenges faced by veterans returning to college. Do any of these sound familiar?

- Having difficulty adjusting to college life
- Having difficulty establishing a support circle and networking effectively
- Becoming easily frustrated
- Feeling on constant alert

Here are some concrete tips to deal with all of these challenges, beginning with patience.

Allow Yourself Time to Adjust

If you were deployed overseas, and especially if you were deployed to a combat zone, you were not sent there the day after you received your orders. Rather, there was a transition period. This probably included pre-deployment and mission-specific training as part of an effort to prepare you for your upcoming duties. In fact, this pre-deployment training may have prevented you from finishing a semester in college or seriously delayed your college plans altogether. Bottom line: This

---

TIP Be sure to identify right away the appropriate resource offices to help you. Most colleges have a Veterans Services office. Make getting to know the staff there a high priority for yourself.

pre-deployment training didn't happen overnight. Besides, even with all of the training and briefings you attended, nothing *really* prepared you for what you experienced in combat, did it?

Similarly, beginning college (or returning to college) following a deployment will also take some time—*give yourself permission to take this time to adjust!* Despite any reintegration briefings you may have received, you will face some challenges in adapting to the college environment. You'll be surrounded by people who simply don't understand what you have experienced while serving your country. The time it takes to adjust is different for everyone, but many veterans report a minimum of one semester, and often a full year, before they felt mostly back to normal.

Part of taking time to adjust is getting comfortable with your new identity as a college student. You may be accustomed to thinking of yourself as "Sergeant Jones," along with all of the accompanying responsibility and authority. Give yourself time to get used to this new identity of a college student, and recognize that it won't happen overnight.

Establish a Support Circle and Combat Isolation

One of the most rewarding experiences in college is making connections with other students. It is important to establish a strong support circle, especially with other people who can relate to your time in the military. This may involve joining or establishing a student-veteran club on campus, where challenges may be openly discussed with others who understand what you've experienced.

This may also include relying on family more often, or making new friends altogether. In the military, you learned to rely on your brothers- and sisters-in-arms to accomplish your mission. In fact, you trusted them with your life—you had their back, and they had yours. Now that you're a civilian again, you should give yourself permission to rely on family for support when you need it. Unlike your past experience in the service where you may have been ordered *not* to talk about your missions, as a college student tasked with balancing family and school responsibilities, it's important to be able to talk to your spouse or family about your concerns. For example, if you have a major research paper due in a week, you may need to ask your husband or wife to shoulder more of the responsibilities—taking care of the kids, bill-paying, working around the house, etc. Just be sure to return the favor and take on some extra responsibility as soon as you are able.

In the military you often had a built-in set of friends. They may have been in your squad or unit, or you may have just worked together on an important mission. To be successful and to gain the most from your college experience, it's important that you're open to forming new friendships. It's not uncommon for students to establish long-term friendships with other students they meet during their first semester on campus, when everyone is struggling with transitioning to college. Besides, your new friend might be just the person to help you as part of a study group preparing for a major exam or someone to brainstorm ideas for that final term paper.

Develop Skills to Deal with Frustration

Whether it's navigating the confusing bureaucracy of a university (which may include an unclear chain of command), interacting with classmates with different priorities, or receiving ambiguous directions from your professor regarding an important assignment, be prepared to experience frustration at times—especially during your first semester following a deployment. Try to remember: Most of your professors and classmates have never experienced the things you have, and they may have a hard time understanding what you've been through. If you're in class listening to an eighteen-year-old complain about her boyfriend back home not calling her often enough, when all you can think about is how stressful it was in Iraq to simply drive down the road, scanning for debris and wondering if an improvised explosive device might injure or kill you or a member of your squad, try to remember that life is all about perspective.

If you start getting frustrated, focus on the fact that it's nothing personal—your classmates aren't intentionally trying to frustrate you, and your professors aren't trying to make your life more stressful. If you're struggling with a class, it's important to remember that your professor has studied their subject for many years and may forget sometimes that, as a new student, you have no knowledge of the subject matter. To avoid this kind of frustration, *give yourself permission to ask for help*. Schedule a meeting with your professor to clarify assignment expectations or talk about study strategies for a major exam. Most faculty are willing to meet with students who need help—they want you to be successful!

Try Not to Be on Constant Alert

Many veterans returning to college report feeling constantly on alert and compelled to watch for threats. Rarely are legitimate threats found in a college classroom. In the military, you were probably trained to instantly react to a threat by attacking that threat with overwhelming force. You need to know in the college environment that it is OK *not* to react if you are challenged by a classmate or professor regarding one of your beliefs or ideas.

Communicating With Faculty and Peers

The ability to develop effective relationships with your professors and other students is a critical skill for success. Here are some strategies for keeping the lines of communication open with peers and faculty.

Schedule Conflicts: Keep Your Professors in the Loop

As a veteran, you may have additional responsibilities that impact your ability to devote as much time to your studies as you would like. For example, you may be in the Army Reserves or National Guard and are required to attend drill one weekend per month. That may not be a problem, unless you have a major exam on the following Monday morning. Developing and maintaining open lines of communication with your faculty members is crucial.

Many faculty members are willing to work with students who have schedule conflicts, particularly if the student has been proactive and informed them well in advance. For example, for National Guard members drill schedules are often published a year in advance. As soon as you receive your syllabus at the beginning of the semester, look closely at the dates exams are scheduled and major assignments are due. If any exam dates fall on the Monday after your drill weekend, immediately schedule an appointment with your professor to discuss your concerns. You may be allowed to take your exam early or make arrangements to take your exam a day later. The important thing is to not wait until just before a test or an assignment is due to ask for an exception, since your professor may interpret this as either laziness or lack of preparation on your part.

> **TIP** People may ask dumb questions. One veteran reported being asked, "How many people did you shoot or kill over there?" Think of several possible responses to inappropriate questions about your military service so you are not caught off guard. Remember, many of your young classmates may not have developed an appropriate filter yet.

Schedule a meeting with an academic adviser and professors early in the semester to discuss:

- VA health care needs, e.g., required VA appointments
- Drill schedule
- Possible conflicts for projects, tests, etc.
- Possible alternatives for achieving course requirements

You can also consult with the Veteran Services office for mediation between academic departments and students.

Group Projects: Learn to Work with Other Students

As part of your college experience, you may occasionally be asked to work on a group project, such as a paper or presentation. Depending on the work ethic and sense of responsibility of your classmates, you may experience frustration when others fail to follow through on assigned tasks, miss deadlines, or simply submit poor quality work. A former marine non-commissioned officer (NCO) described having to reset her expectations when working with traditional-age college students. As an NCO, she was accustomed to taking charge, tasking assignments, and expecting everyone to perform their duties to the best of their ability. However, she quickly found her strong leadership style was not always appreciated by her classmates. She discovered she needed to allow other students to take leadership roles.

Take Advantage of Veteran Support Services

Just like the U.S. military, higher education has a complicated bureaucracy and you must learn to successfully navigate your way through it. Fortunately, most campuses have a variety of resources available to help you.

Find Important Offices on Campus

On-campus offices offer a wide range of services to student veterans. Keep in mind that the exact names of these offices may be different at your school, but you can use your school's Web site to find out what they're called on your campus.

Veteran Services Office. Many colleges are adopting a one-stop-shop approach for providing services to veteran students. This department likely includes a VA certifying official and may include staff to help you navigate the complexities of your GI bill and other financial aid issues. You might also get help in enrolling for classes and understanding the restrictions on repeating courses within the requirements of the GI bill. Additionally, you may find contact information for academic advising, career counseling, specialized counseling services, and veteran student peer advisers or mentors.

Be sure to schedule an appointment at this office and to bring a list of questions. Here are some to begin with:

1. What paperwork will I need to expedite processing?
2. How long before I receive my benefits or financial aid?
3. Will my GI bill benefits affect my eligibility for additional financial aid?
4. Are there additional veteran-student advocates on campus, and if so, who are they and how may I contact them?

Academic Advisement. Think of your academic adviser as one of the most important people you will meet on campus. Your adviser can help you select appropriate classes for your major, understand important policies and procedures, connect you with campus resources, and serve as a mentor.

Career Services Office. This office can help you translate your military training into transferable skills appropriate for the civilian world, provide assistance with developing résumés, give mock-interviews, help you explore career choices, and much more.

Division of Student Affairs. Offices within this division can help you learn about opportunities to get involved in campus life and student organizations, volunteer service opportunities, campus housing options, and ways for you and your family to participate in activities and events.

Financial Aid Office. This office can help you understand your options for financial aid, including grants, loans, scholarship opportunities, and work-study options. Often these offices have a designated veteran services liaison to assist you with the complexities of GI bill funding, short-term loans to accommodate delays in veteran aid processing, and other issues.

TIP Did you know that many colleges and universities may allow you to count some of your military training as transfer credits? Talk with your admissions counselor or transfer adviser to see if your institution does.

Tutoring Centers. Many campuses have centralized support services to assist students with math and writing skills development. Find out where these resources are on your campus and take full advantage of them. Some colleges even have specialized services for veterans (e.g., veteran tutors to help other veteran students).

Veterans' Voices ‖ How I Became a Successful Student Veteran

Case Study #1   Marine Corps Reservist: *John,* Senior at Missouri State University

"I've been in the Marine Reserves while I was in college. I was deployed for 13 months, with five of those months in Iraq. I missed the second half of my sophomore year during my train-up, and my whole junior year."

- **Be prepared for culture shock.** "You'll be going from the highly structured military environment to the totally unstructured environment of college. Sometimes having so much freedom to spend your time any way you want can be a bad thing—at least until you figure things out. It's important to be able to provide structure for yourself now, since no one will be doing it for you."

- **Give yourself time to adjust.** "With the Marine Corps Reserves, I literally went from being on patrol in Afghanistan one week to being back in college the next—and I was already two weeks behind in my classes when I got back. It's going to take some time to get used to everything again, before you feel like yourself. Just expect it will be tough for a while, but know that you'll get through it. It took me about a semester before I felt like—mostly—my old self."

- **Talk to your professors early and often.** "As a reservist, there are times I'm required to do training, and I have absolutely no control over that schedule. Be sure you talk to your professors as soon as you know your training schedule, so you can deal with schedule conflicts early. I've found most faculty members to be very understanding, and several have let me take exams early or have given me an extension on a paper because I had to be away for training."

Get Help with Mental Health Issues

It is not uncommon, particularly for combat veterans, to experience some mental health challenges upon returning home. One of the most common problems is post-traumatic stress disorder (PTSD). The symptoms of PTSD often start within three months of a traumatic event, although sometimes may not appear for several years. Symptoms typically last longer than several weeks and may cause significant disruption in your ability to do well in college and life outside school.

SYMPTOMS OF PTSD

- Difficulty sleeping, including nightmares
- Disturbing thoughts, including flashbacks
- Feelings of guilt
- Feeling depressed or worrying excessively
- Memory problems and trouble concentrating
- Being easily startled or feeling on edge
- Anger outbursts
- Self-destructive behavior, like drinking too much
- Losing interest in activities enjoyed in the past

Symptoms such as those previously described will negatively impact your ability to focus on your studies and should be addressed as soon as possible.

WHERE TO GO FOR HELP

Fortunately, most colleges and universities have personnel and resources to help. These may include a counseling center, support groups, and a health center staffed by physicians and other health care providers. With large numbers of veterans returning to college, more counseling centers are employing counselors trained to assist the unique needs of these students. If the campus counseling center is unable to provide expertise in this area, you may be referred to a community agency or veteran health care facility that may be better equipped to assist you.

**Case Study #2   Army National Guard Soldier: *Kevin*,
                              Sophomore at Missouri State University**

"I've been in the National Guard since high school and was deployed to Afghanistan last year. I've missed about a year and a half of college . . . but that's OK, because I'm a much better student now than when I left."

- **Support circles are important.** "It's really important to surround yourself with family and friends, especially the first semester after a deployment. For me, after my tour in Iraq I didn't really fit in with my fraternity brothers anymore, so family is more important than ever."

- **Identity issues and the power divide.** "I had to keep reminding myself I was 'only' a college student now like everyone else. I was an E-5 in the Army, and I had a lot of responsibility. I was accustomed to taking charge and making things happen. Now, as a college student, I had to re-evaluate my position, like on this group project for a class. I couldn't believe a couple of the other students didn't do their assigned work, which really caused the rest of the group a lot of stress."

- **Figure out your priorities to accomplish your mission.** "Before my deployment, I spent too much time partying. I had a lot of fun, but my grades weren't so great. Now that I'm back, I'm a lot more focused on school, which has really helped my grades. I decided graduating with a high GPA was my new mission . . . after that, things just kind of fell into place."

Final Words of Advice

All branches of the armed services require some kind of basic training or boot camp. This training provides the basic knowledge and skills necessary to perform required duties and also to learn about the culture and customs of the military. You might think of the first semester following a deployment as your boot camp for college success. You may need to relearn many of the study skills you previously took for granted, and you also may need to allow yourself time to refamiliarize yourself with campus culture and customs.

Effectively utilizing all available campus and community resources and communicating early and often with your professors and other key

Tips for Success
• Reestablish important relationships and renegotiate roles with family members.
• Realize that controlling emotions requires *both* holding in *and* expressing emotions appropriately.
• Develop good academic habit and study skills.
• Utilize available campus resources, especially those designed for veterans.
• Try to find opportunities to talk about wartime experiences and transition challenges.
• Maintain physical fitness.
• Limit use of alcohol and illegal substances.
• Minimize exposure to war-related news reports.
• Take time to grieve for and honor others who were lost.

campus personnel are important first steps. As a returning veteran, you might consider using your experiences to help other student veterans by becoming a student mentor. You can serve as a role model for new students by sharing your life experience and leadership skills and offer support to other veterans struggling with transitioning to college. Tutor other veterans in math or writing if you did well in those classes. Identify veteran-friendly faculty on campus, and share that information with your fellow veterans and Veteran Services office.

Additional Veterans' Resources

The American Legion. The nation's largest wartime veterans service organization. **www.legion.org**

Department of Veterans Affairs. The U.S. government site for veteran services. **www.va.gov/**

DD 214 Online request. A site to access military records. **www.archives.gov/veterans/military-service-records/**

Federal Benefits for Veteran's Book. Outlines benefits for veterans, dependents, and survivors. **www.va.gov/opa/publications/benefits_book.asp**

Iraq and Afghanistan Veterans of America. The first and largest nonprofit, nonpartisan organization for Iraq and Afghanistan veterans. **http://iava.org/**

Military.com. Resources for members of all branches of U.S. Armed Forces and their families. **www.military.com**

Student Veterans of America. Provides military veterans with the resources, support, and advocacy needed to succeed in higher education and following graduation. **www.studentveterans.org/**

TRICARE: Health care program for uniformed service members, retirees, and their families worldwide. **www.tricare.mil/**

U.S. Department of Veteran Affairs Educational Services. Outlines the educational benefits provided to veterans. **www.gibill.va.gov/**

United States Marine Corp Wounded Warrior Regiment. Provides assistance to wounded, ill, and injured Marines. **www.woundedwarriorregiment.org/**

Veterans Network. A country-wide directory of veterans groups. **www.veteransnetwork.net/directory.php**

Bibliography

Ackerman, Robert, David DiRamio, and Regina Mitchell."Transitions: CombatVeterans as College Students."*New Directions for Student Services* 126 (2009): 5–14. Print.

Summerlot, John, Sean-Michael Green, and Daniel Parker. (2009). "Student veterans organizations." *New Directions for Student Services* 126 (2009): 71–79. Print.

"Post-traumatic stress disorder." *Mayo Clinic.* Mayo Foundation for Medical Education and Research (MFMER), n.d. Web. 19 Oct. 2012 **<www.mayoclinic.com/health/post-traumatic-stress-disorder/ DS00246/DSECTION=symptoms>**.